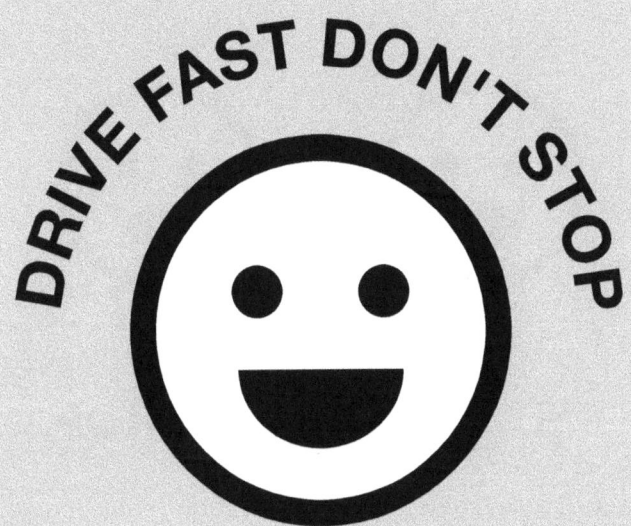

DRIVE FAST DON'T STOP

2

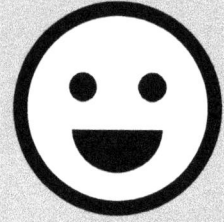
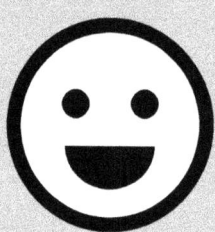

# DRIVE FAST DON'T STOP

BOOK TWO

LAMBO
FERRARI
PORSCHE

FAST DON'T

FAST DON'T

E FAST DON'T

VE FAST DON'T ST

RIVE FAST DON'T STO

DRIVE FAST DON'T STOP

DRIVE FAST DON'T STOP

DRIVE FAST DON'T STOP

LAMBO

LAMBO

LAMBO

LAMBO

LAMBO

LAMBO

LAMBO

LAMBO

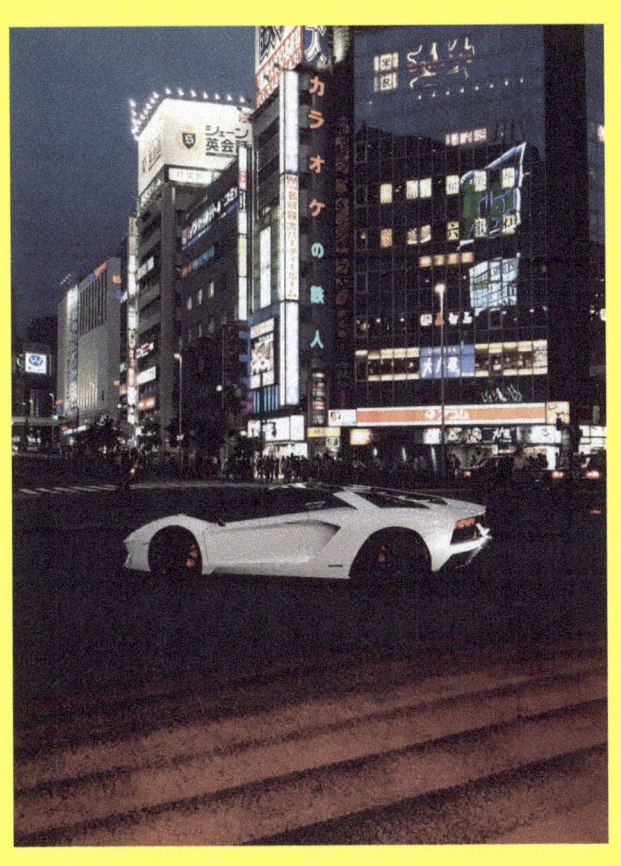

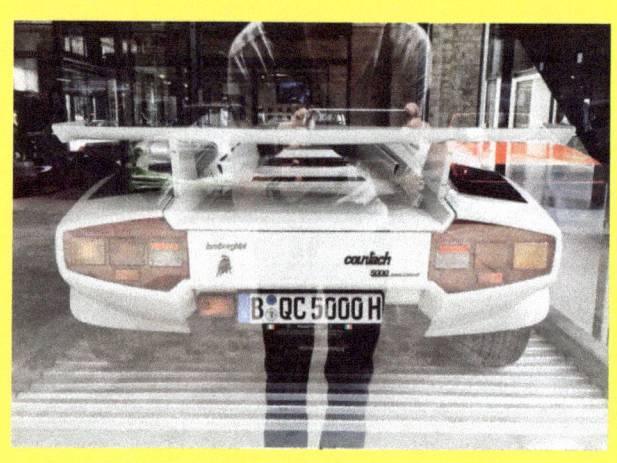

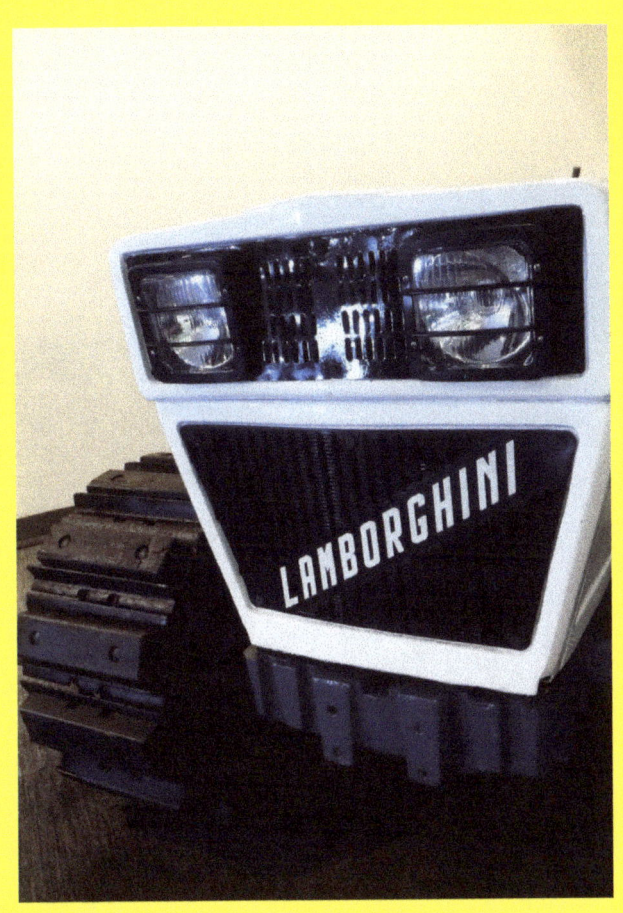

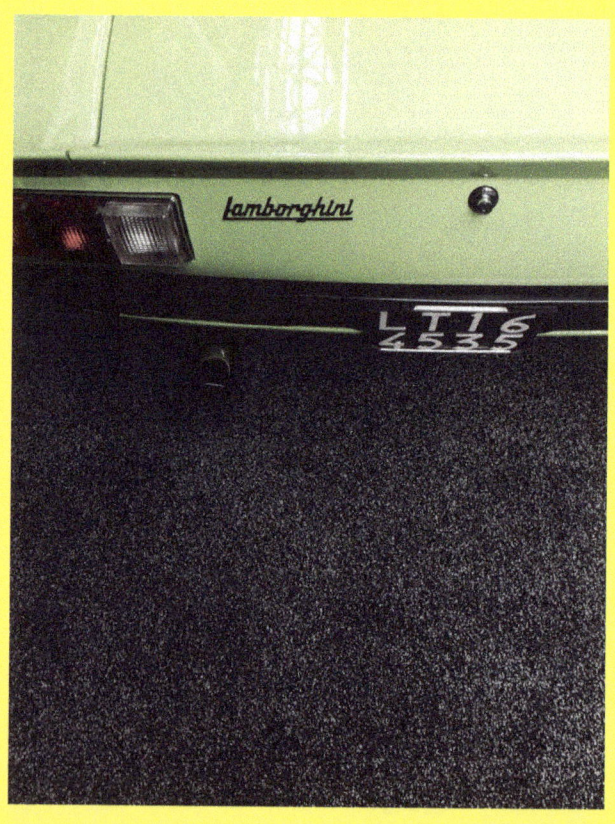

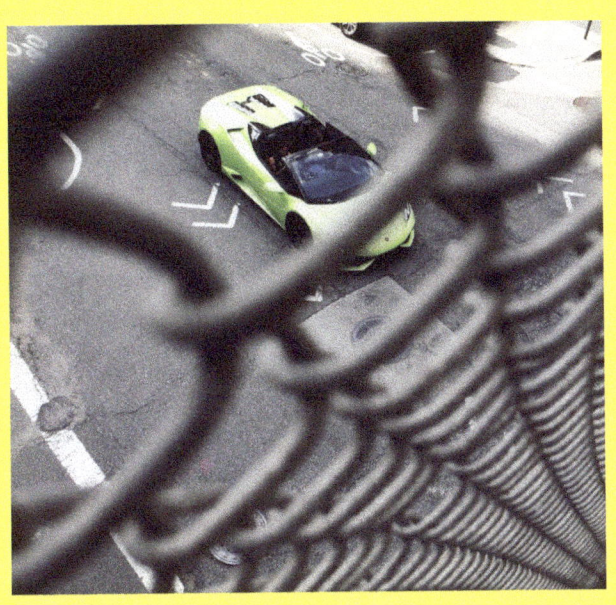

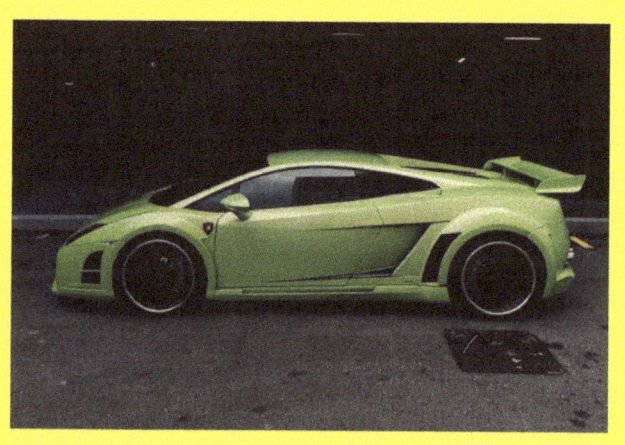

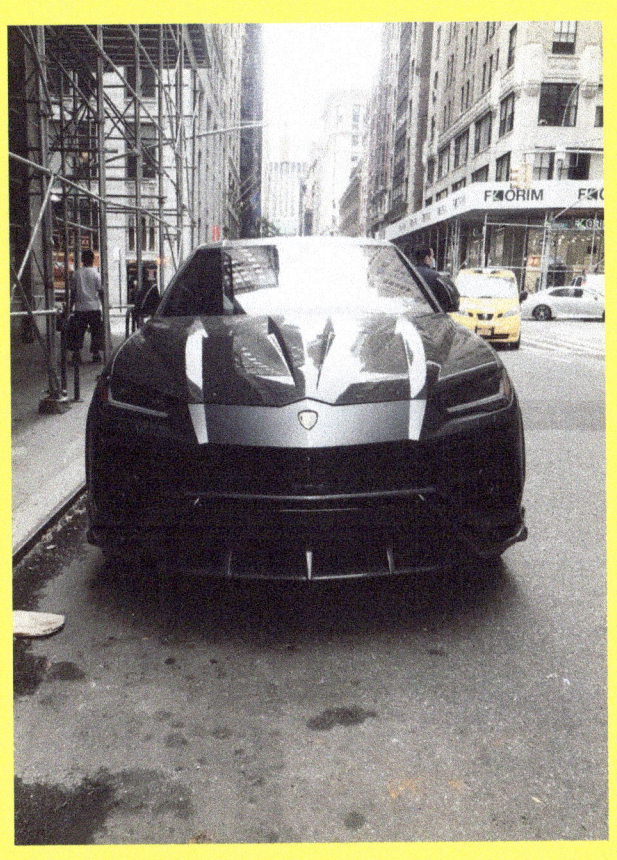

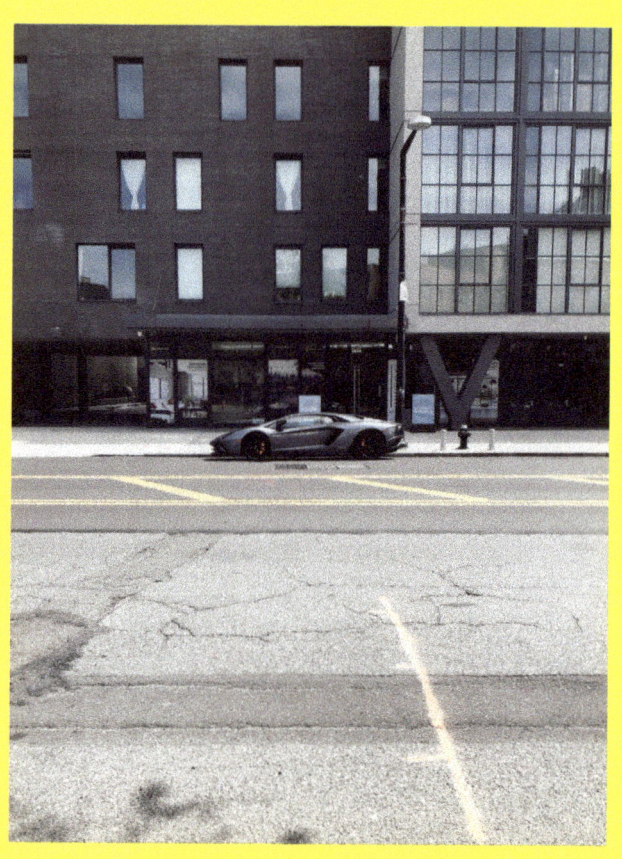

# FERRARI

FERRARI

FERRARI

FERRARI

FERRARI

FERRARI

FERRARI

FERRARI

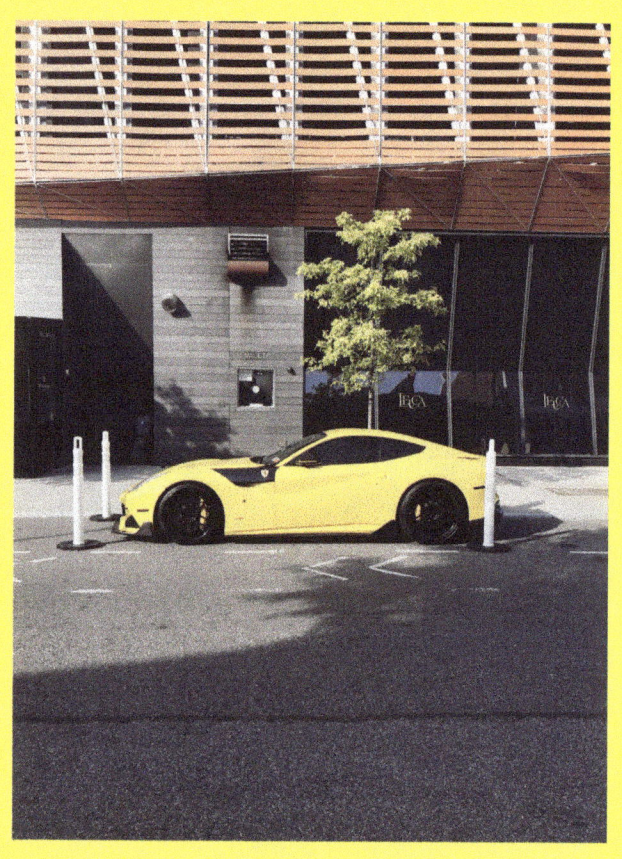

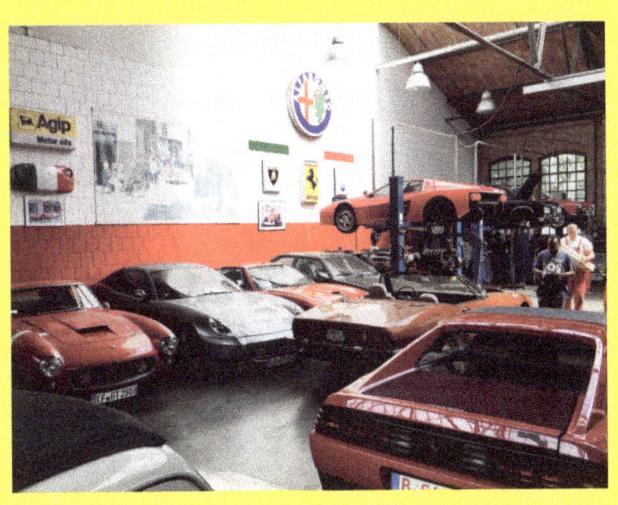

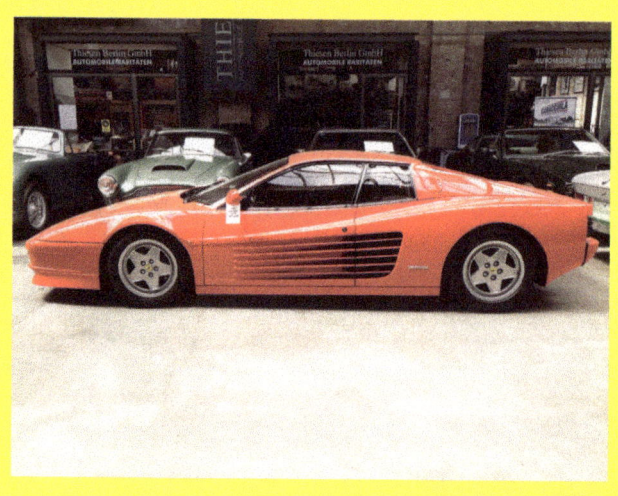

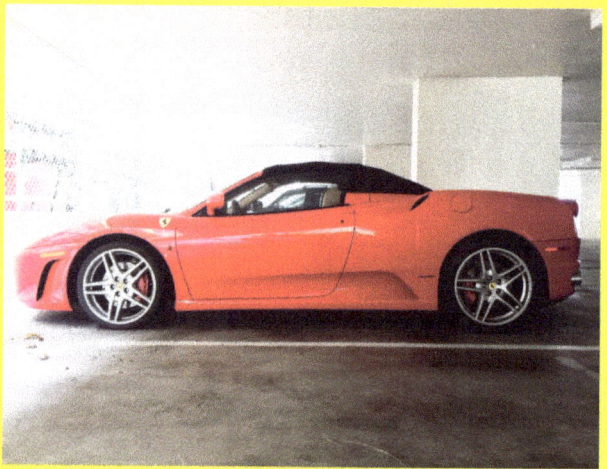

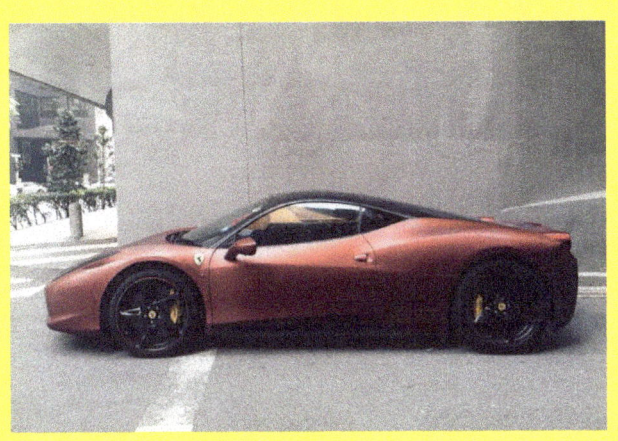

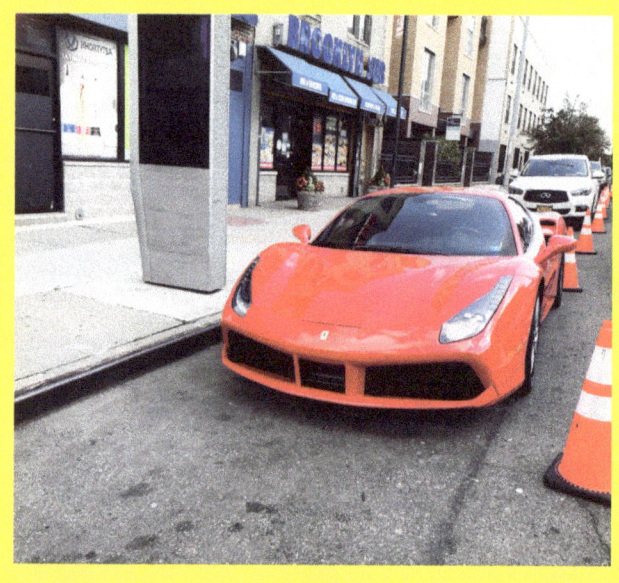

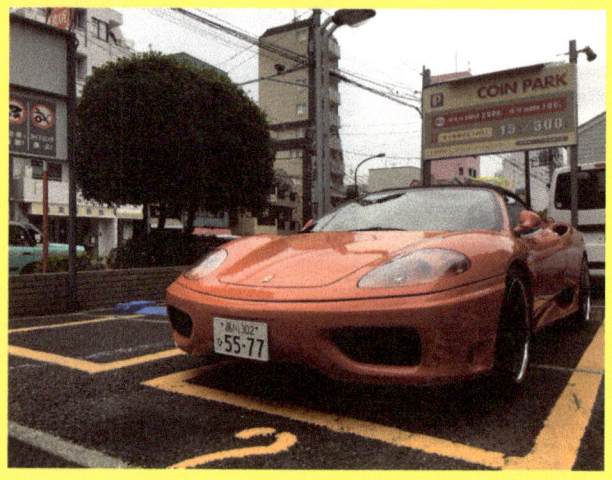

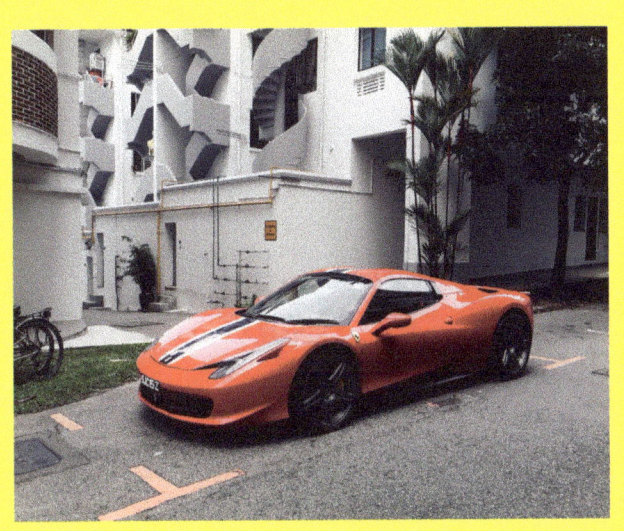

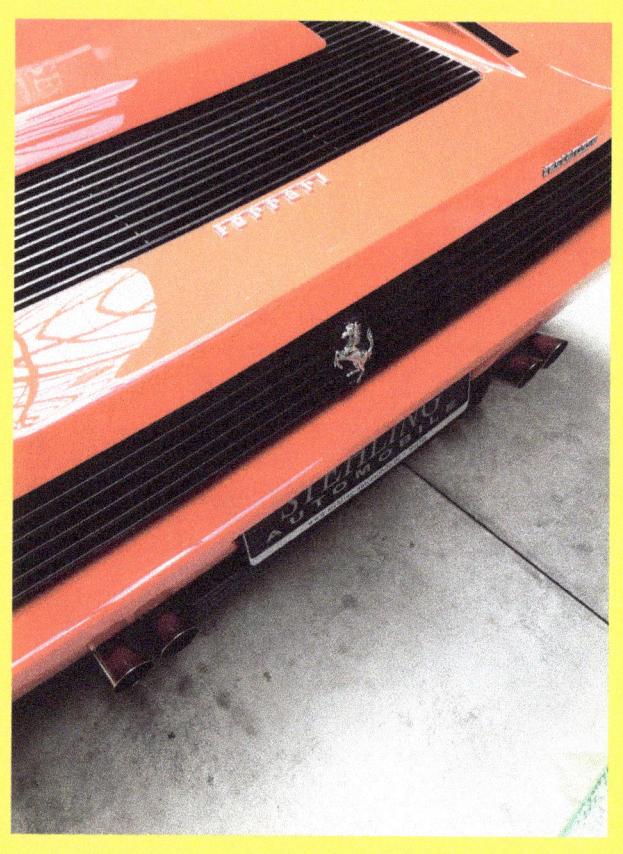

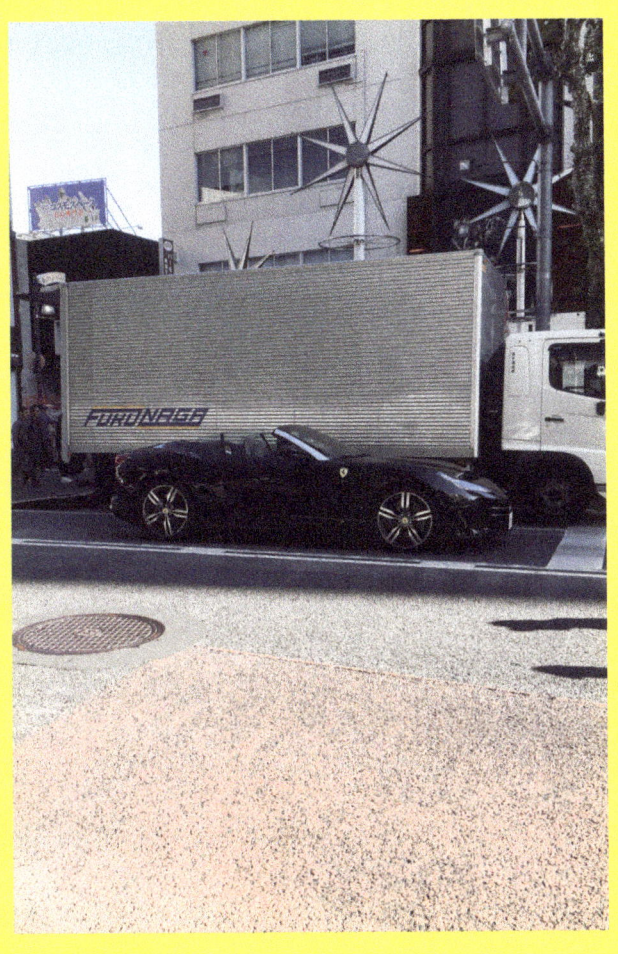

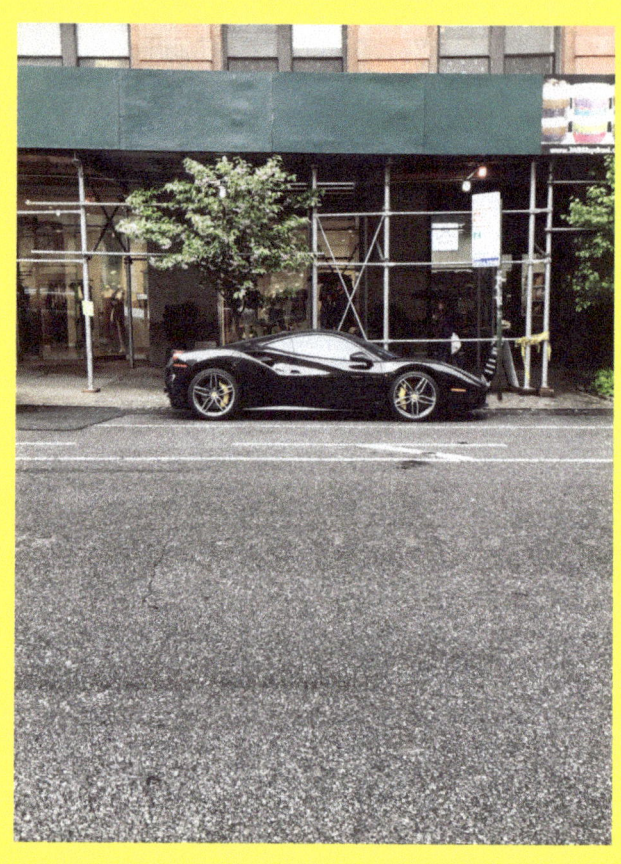

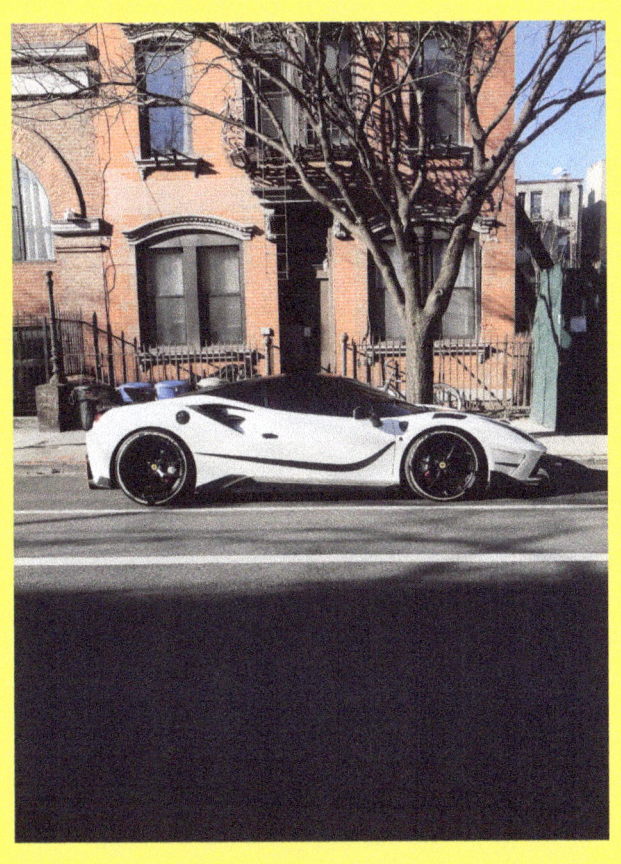

# PORSCHE

# PORSCHE

# PORSCHE

## PORSCHE

### PORSCHE

#### PORSCHE

PORSCHE

PORSCHE

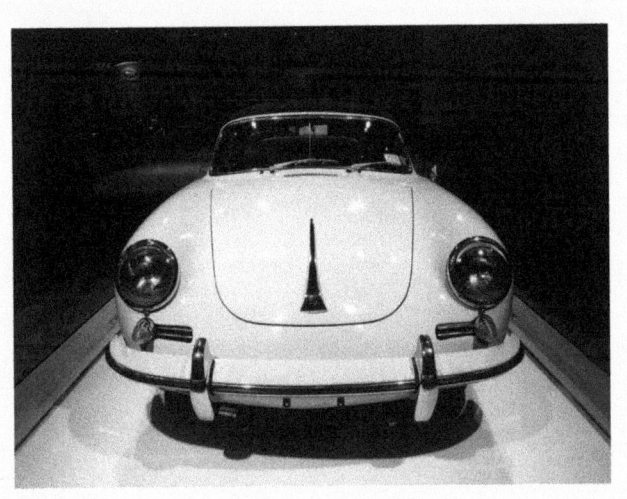

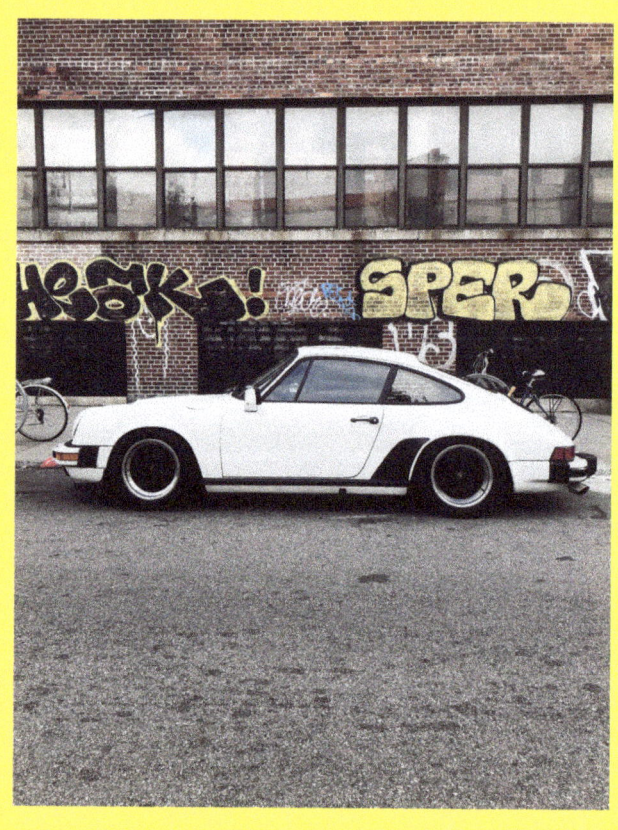

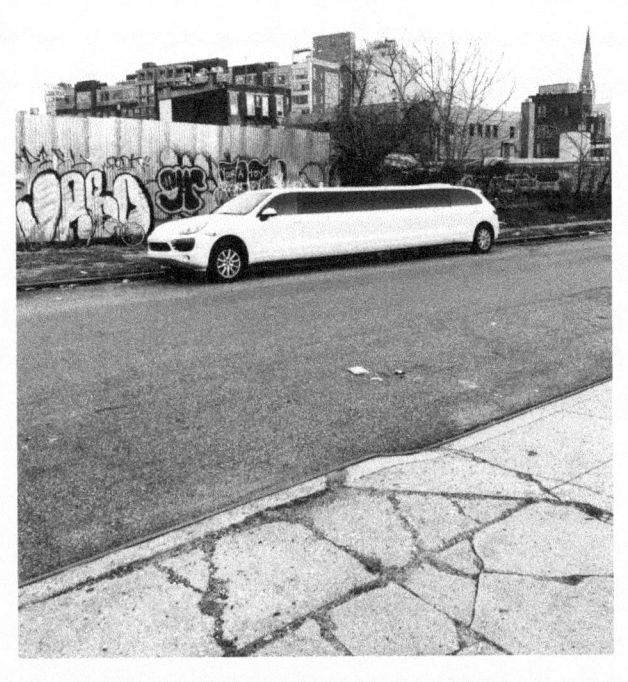

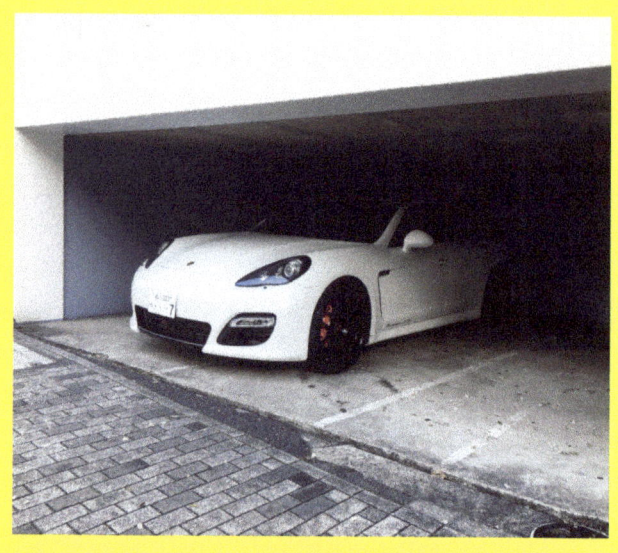

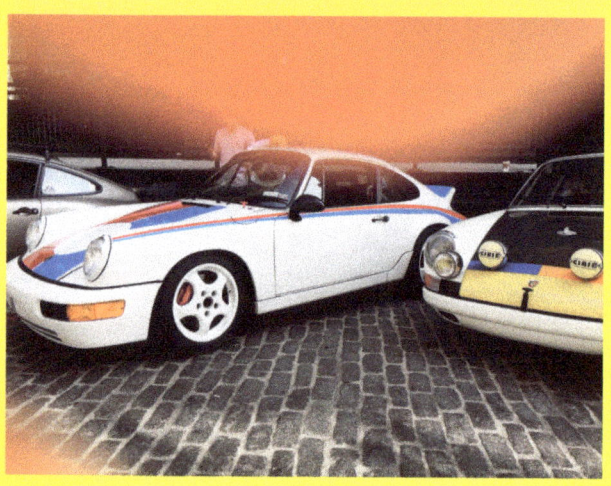

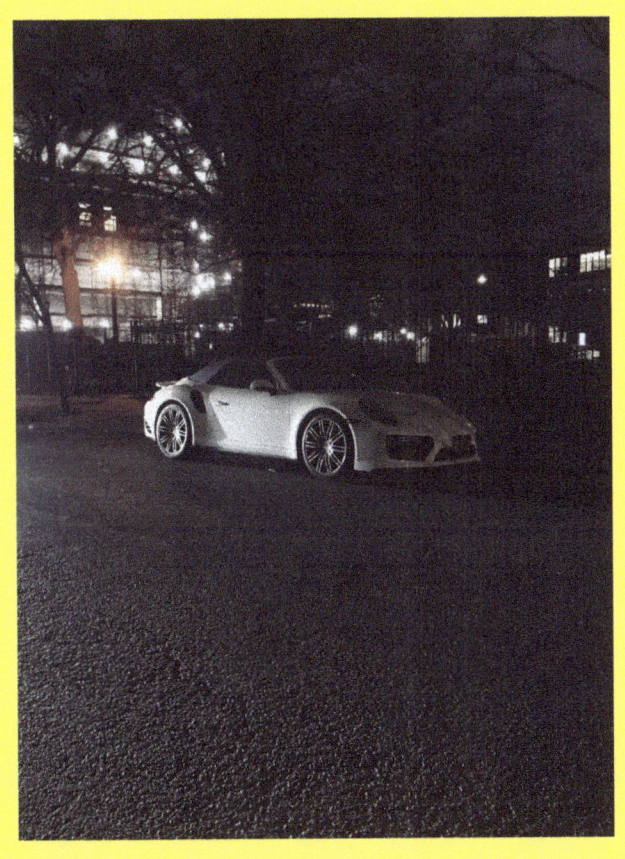

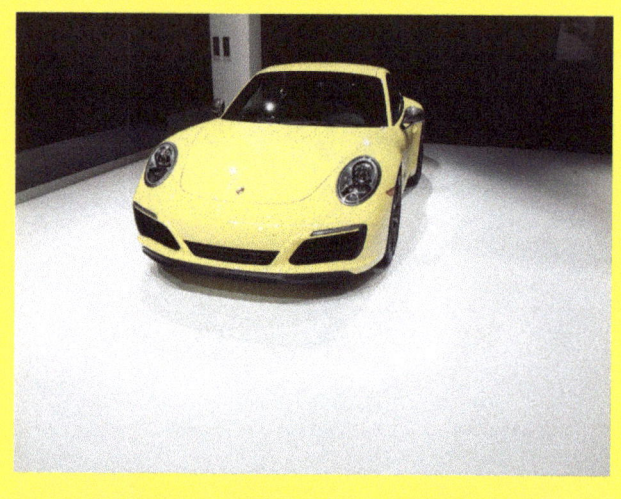

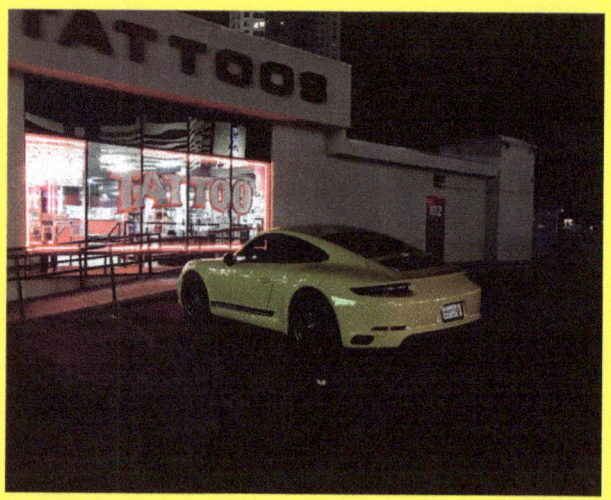

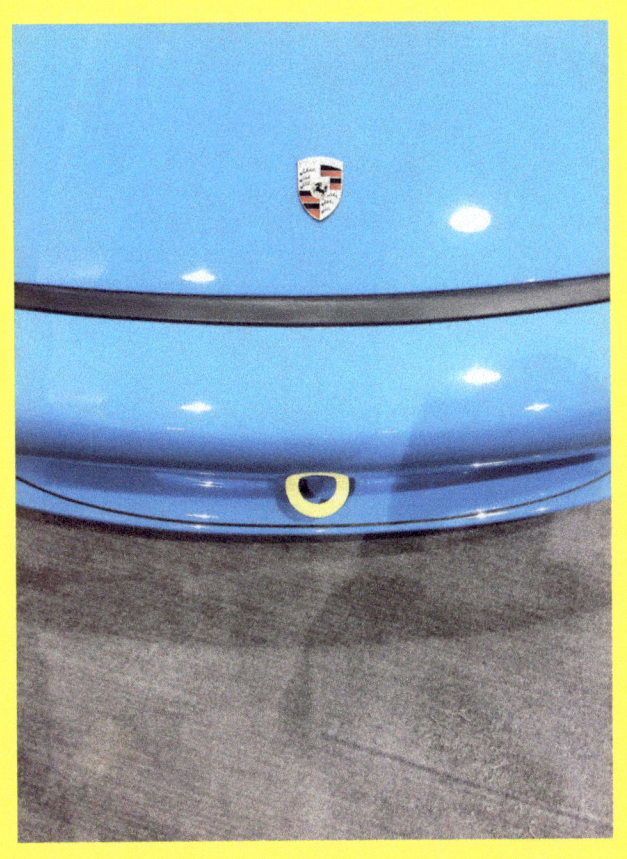

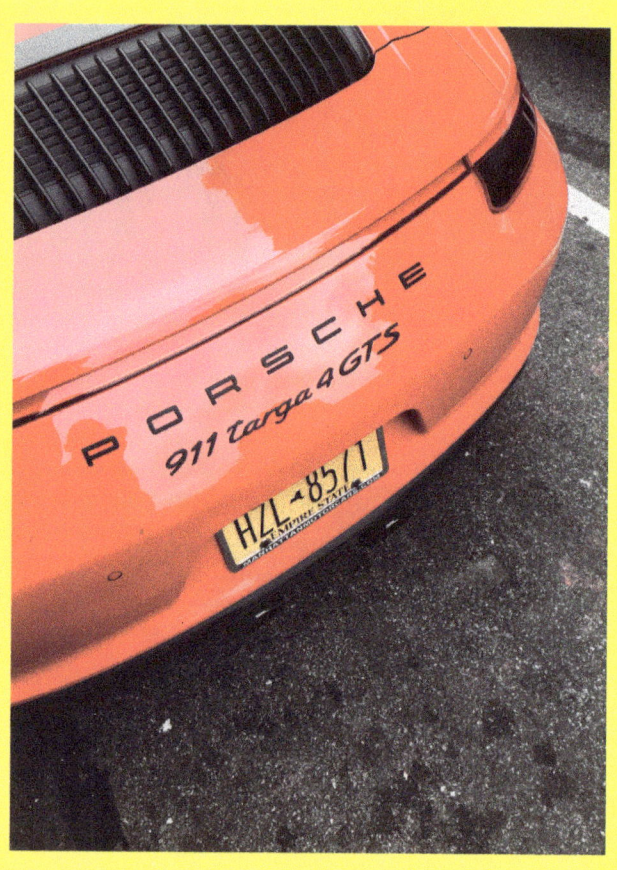

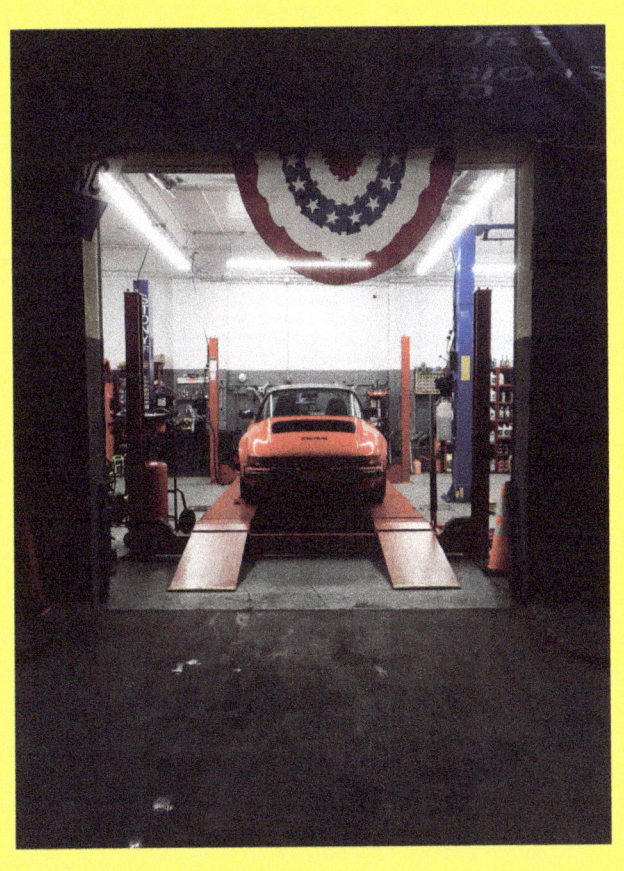

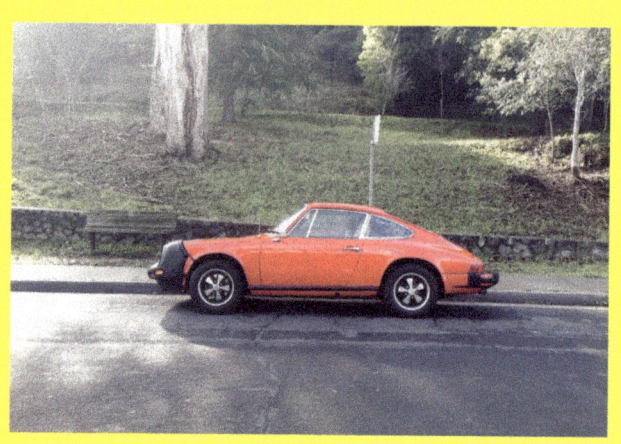

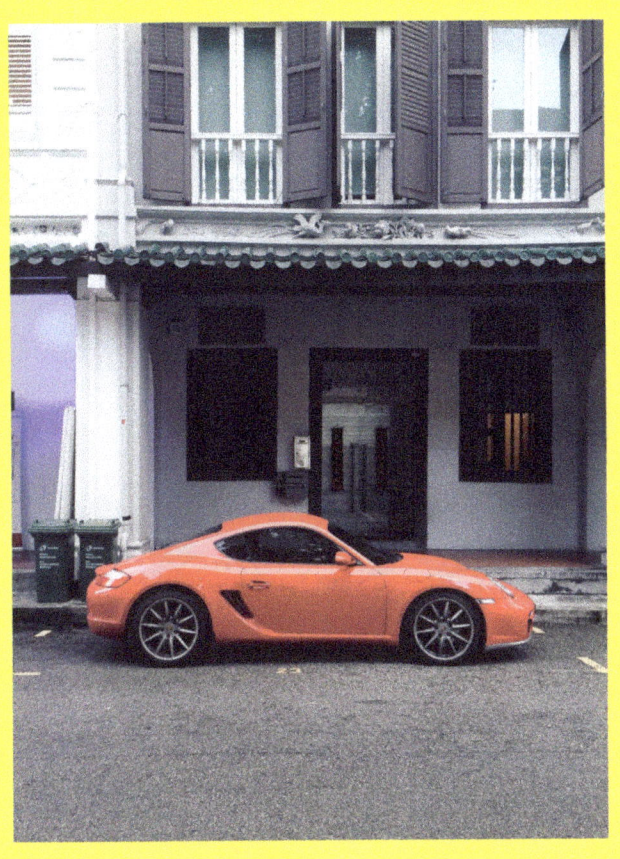

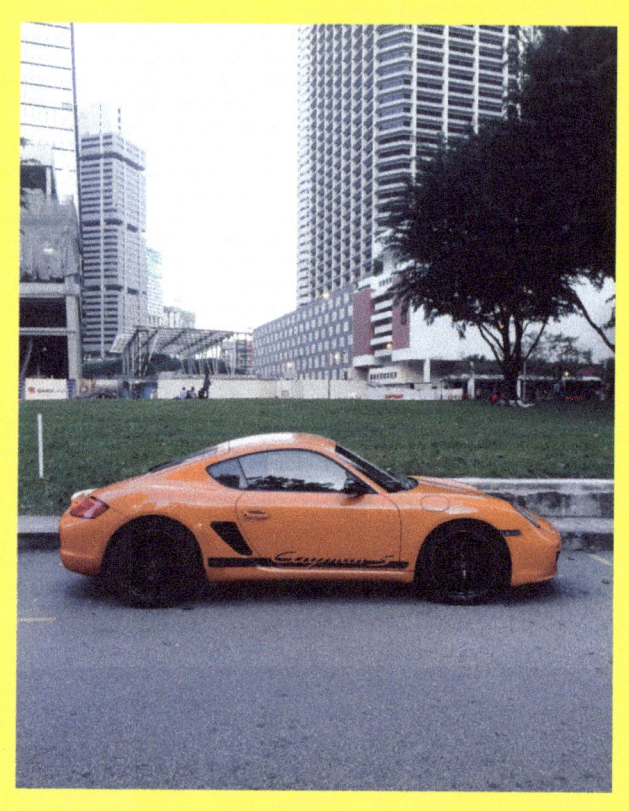

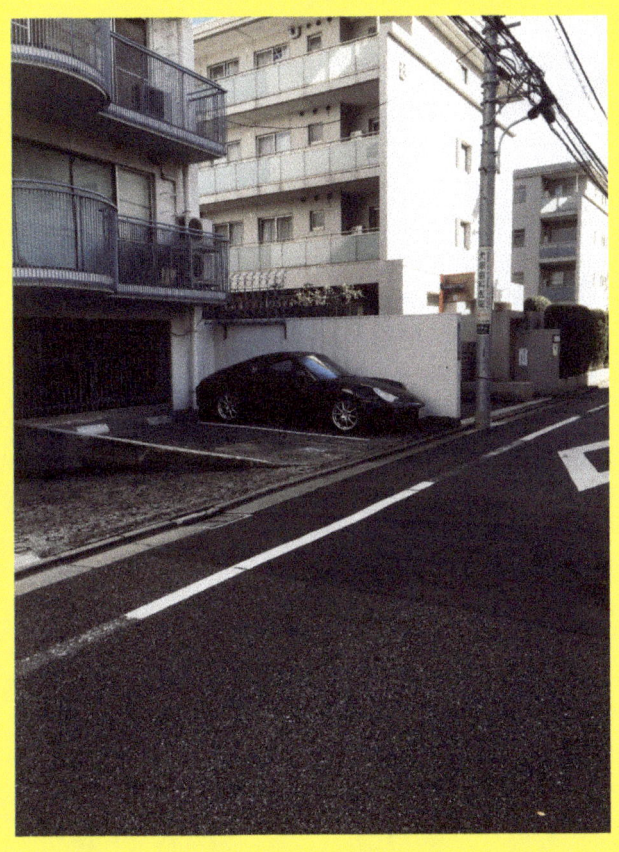

END

END

END

END

END

END

END

END

FAST DON"

FAST DON'T

E FAST DON'T

VE FAST DON'T ST

RIVE FAST DON'T STO

DRIVE FAST DON'T STOP

DRIVE FAST DON'T STOP

DRIVE FAST DON'T STOP

# DRIVE FAST DON'T STOP

AUTOMOTIVE PHOTO ARCHIVE
BY
MATTHEW JOCELYN

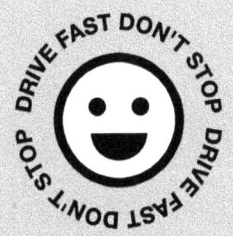

**2**